0 2 MAY 2019

This book is on loan from
Library Services for Schools
www.cumbria.gov.uk/
libraries/schoolslibserv

County Council

ENDANGERED ANIMALS

AFRICA

by
Grace Jones

Image Credits

All images are courtesy of Shutterstock.com, unless otherwise specified. With thanks to Getty Images, Thinkstock Photo and iStockphoto.
Front Cover – ShaunWilkinson, Sergey Uryadnikov, JacoBecker. 1 – Andrzej Kubik. 4&5 – Iakov Filimonov, Andrej Antic, Reinhold Leitner. 6&7 – Rainer Plendl, Ivan Karpov, Donovan van Staden, Artur Balytskyi, Mopic. 8&9 – Volodymyr Burdiak. 10&11 – Donovan van Staden, ArCaLu, mareandmare, Kletr, Roman Samokhin, Butterfly Hunter, Svetlana Foote, Vladimir Wrangel, Steve Collender, Eric Isselee. 12&13 – Michael Potter11, Svetlana Foote, W. Scott McGill. 14&15 – Mike Price, Qiuyun Song, LMspencer. 16&17 – NaturesMomentsuk, Michele Alfieri, PhotocechCZ. 18&19 – PicturesWild, Chris Humphries, Michael Potter11. 20&21 – Maggy Meyer. 22&23 – Eric Gevaert, cybercrisi, Sergey Uryadnikov. 24&25 – evenfh, Attila JANDI, sirtravelalot. 26&27 – Even Look, Thitsanu Angkapunyadech, shaferaphoto, Bildagentur Zoonar GmbH, Juliya Shangarey, SpeedKingz. 29 – Kiki Dohmeier, Four Oaks, Claude Huot, ArCaLu, Michael Potter11, Patrick Goersch.

BookLife
PUBLISHING

©2018
BookLife Publishing
King's Lynn
Norfolk PE30 4LS

A catalogue record for this book is available from the British Library.

ISBN: 978-1-78637-248-2

Written by:
Grace Jones

Edited by:
Holly Duhig

Designed by:
Drue Rintoul

CONTENTS

Words that look like this are explained in the glossary on page 30.

ENDANGERED ANIMALS

Experts estimate that there are anywhere between two million and nine million **species** living on planet Earth today, but thousands of these are in danger of dying out every single year.

Polar Bear

WHAT DOES IT MEAN IF A SPECIES IS ENDANGERED?

Any species of plant or animal that is at risk of dying out completely is said to be endangered. When all individuals of a single species die, that species has become extinct. Extinction is a real possibility for all species that are already threatened or endangered. Experts estimate that between 150 and 200 different species become extinct every day.

Dinosaurs are an example of an extinct species. They walked the Earth over 225 million years ago and became extinct around 65 million years ago.

The International Union for Conservation of Nature and Natural Resources (IUCN) is the main **organisation** that records which species are in danger of extinction. The species are put into different categories, from the most to the least threatened by extinction.

IUCN'S CATEGORIES OF THREATENED ANIMALS

Category	Explanation
Extinct	Species that have no surviving members
Extinct in the Wild	Species with surviving members only in **captivity**
Critically Endangered	Species that have an extremely high risk of extinction in the wild
Endangered	Species that have a high risk of extinction in the wild
Vulnerable	Species that are likely to become endangered or critically endangered in the near future
Near Threatened	Species that are likely to become vulnerable or endangered in the near future
Least Concern	Species that fit into none of the above categories

The IUCN's work is extremely important. Once a species has been recognised as 'at risk', organisations and **governments** will often take steps to protect the species and its **habitats** in order to save it from extinction. The practice of protecting or saving a species and its habitats is called **conservation**.

The Javan rhinoceros has been categorised by the IUCN as 'critically endangered', with around 46-66 individuals remaining in the wild.

5

WHY DO ANIMALS BECOME ENDANGERED?

Over the last 100 years, the human **population** of the world has grown by over 4.5 billion people. As the population has grown, the damage humans do to the **environment** and wildlife has increased too. Many experts believe that human activity is the biggest threat to animals around the world today.

Habitat Destruction

One of the biggest threats species face is the loss of their habitats. Large areas of land are often used to build **settlements** to provide more housing, food and **natural resources** for the growing world population. This can often destroy natural habitats, which nearby wildlife need in order to survive.

To use land for housing or farming, all the trees must be cut down and cleared from the area. This is called **deforestation**.

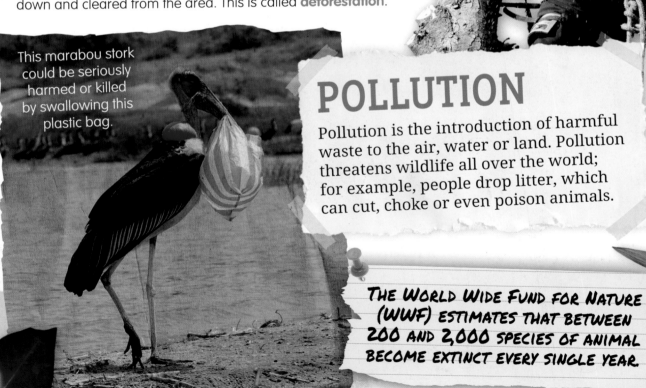

This marabou stork could be seriously harmed or killed by swallowing this plastic bag.

POLLUTION

Pollution is the introduction of harmful waste to the air, water or land. Pollution threatens wildlife all over the world; for example, people drop litter, which can cut, choke or even poison animals.

THE WORLD WIDE FUND FOR NATURE (WWF) ESTIMATES THAT BETWEEN 200 AND 2,000 SPECIES OF ANIMAL BECOME EXTINCT EVERY SINGLE YEAR.

Hunters and Poachers

Many species are endangered because of hunting or **poaching**. Humans throughout history have hunted certain species of animal for their meat, furs, skins or tusks.

Male African elephants are hunted by poachers for their huge tusks, which are made from a natural material called ivory and are sold for lots of money.

The dodo was a species of bird that was hunted to extinction. The last time a dodo was seen alive was in 1662.

Natural Causes

While the most serious threats to animals are caused by humans, there are natural threats to animals too. For example, it is thought that the extinction of the dinosaurs was caused by a natural event, when a **meteorite** hit the Earth. Other species may become extinct because they are not as well **adapted** to survive in their environments as others. Experts believe that the number of species that become extinct due to human activity is around 1,000 times more than those becoming extinct through natural causes.

AFRICA

Africa is one of the seven continents of the world. Continents are large areas of land that, along with the five oceans, make up the Earth's surface. The other six continents are: Antarctica, Asia, Australia, Europe, North America and South America. Africa is the second largest continent in the world. It is located to the south of Europe and Asia, and north of Antarctica. There are two oceans that surround Africa. The South Atlantic Ocean lies on the west coast of Africa and the Indian Ocean lies on the south-east coast.

CONTINENTS OF THE WORLD

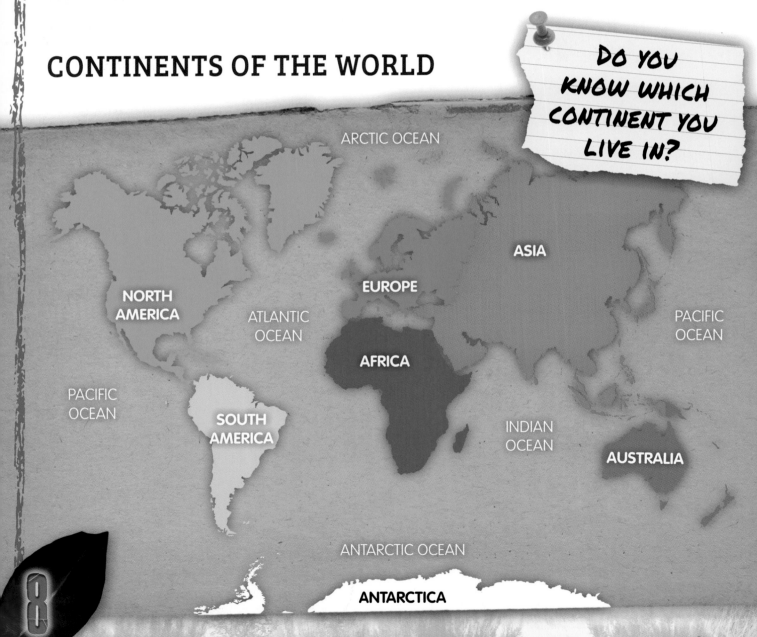

DO YOU KNOW WHICH CONTINENT YOU LIVE IN?

ARCTIC OCEAN

ASIA

EUROPE

NORTH AMERICA

ATLANTIC OCEAN

PACIFIC OCEAN

AFRICA

PACIFIC OCEAN

SOUTH AMERICA

INDIAN OCEAN

AUSTRALIA

ANTARCTIC OCEAN

ANTARCTICA

FACTS ABOUT AFRICA

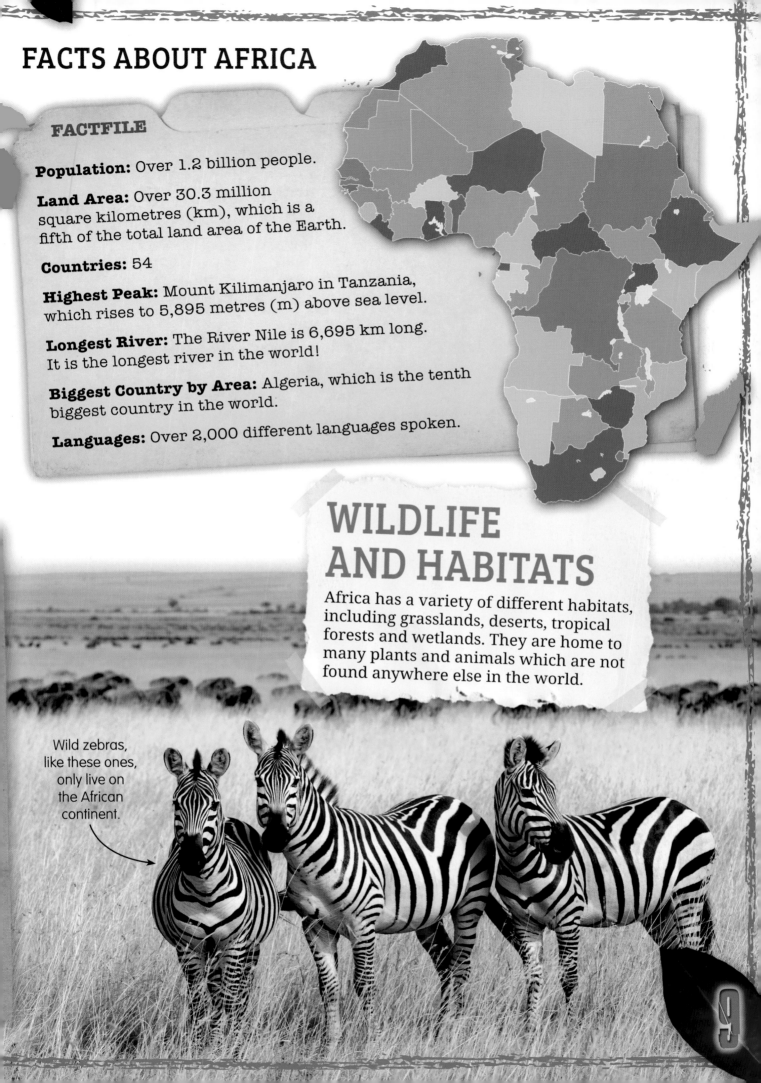

WILDLIFE AND HABITATS

Africa has a variety of different habitats, including grasslands, deserts, tropical forests and wetlands. They are home to many plants and animals which are not found anywhere else in the world.

Wild zebras, like these ones, only live on the African continent.

ENDANGERED AFRICAN ANIMALS

Some of the biggest threats facing Africa's wildlife today are: the effects of population growth, habitat destruction, poaching and hunting. Poaching in particular has affected some of the continent's wildlife because many African species are prized for their valuable fur, skin or tusks. It is estimated that there are around 1,350 species in danger in Africa.

10 ANIMALS IN DANGER IN AFRICA

1

African Elephant

Conservation Status:
Vulnerable

Number:
Around 415,000

2

Ethiopian Wolf

Conservation Status:
Endangered

Number:
Less than 500

3

Northern White Rhino

Conservation Status:
Extinct in the Wild

Number:
3 in Captivity

4

African Lion

Conservation Status:
Vulnerable

Number:
Less than 30,000

5

Mountain Gorilla

Conservation Status:
Critically Endangered

Number:
Around 880

6

African Penguin

Conservation Status:
Endangered

Number:
Around 50,000

7

Cheetah

Conservation Status:
Vulnerable

Number:
Around 6,700

8

Grevy's Zebra

Conservation Status:
Endangered

Number:
Less than 2,000

9

Black Rhinoceros

Conservation Status:
Critically Endangered

Number:
Between 5,000 – 5,500

10

Chimpanzee

Conservation Status:
Endangered

Number:
Around 300,000

AFRICAN ELEPHANT

FACTFILE

Number Living in the Wild: Around 415,000

IUCN Status: Vulnerable

Scientific Name: *Loxodonta africana*

Weight: 3,500 to 6,500 kilograms (kg)

Size: Up to 3.4 m

Life Span: 60 to 70 years

Habitat: Savannah, grassland, desert and rainforest

Diet: Herbivore

A male African elephant, like this one shown here, is called a bull and a female is called a cow.

Where Do They Live?

African elephants live in a variety of habitats all across Africa including savannahs, grasslands, deserts and rainforests.

Key

Oceans and Seas
Land
Elephant Habitats

AFRICA

Indian Ocean

Atlantic Ocean

WHY ARE THEY IN DANGER?

Since 1986, the IUCN has listed the African elephant as in danger. The biggest threat to the species comes from poaching. Poachers **illegally** kill African elephants for their tusks, which are made from ivory and are extremely valuable. The ivory tusks are sold at high prices and are mostly used to make carvings.

A pile of illegally poached ivory tusks.

How Are They Being Protected?

In December 2016, the Convention for International Trade in Endangered Species (CITES) agreed to ban the **domestic** ivory trade in all of the 183 countries who are members of the organisation. This includes China, which has the largest domestic ivory market in the whole world. Many people hope that this ban may save the African elephant from extinction in the future.

EACH YEAR, POACHERS KILL OVER 8% OF THE TOTAL POPULATION OF AFRICAN ELEPHANTS. AT THIS RATE, ELEPHANTS MAY BECOME EXTINCT WITHIN THE NEXT TEN YEARS.

This statue has been carved from elephant tusks.

13

MOUNTAIN GORILLA

FACTFILE

Number Living in the Wild: Around 880

IUCN Status: Critically Endangered

Scientific Name: *Gorilla beringei beringei*

Weight: Males weigh up to 185 kg and females up to 100 kg

Size: 1.5 to 1.8 m

Life Span: 40 to 50 years

Habitat: Mountain habitats or bamboo forests that are at high **altitudes**

Diet: Herbivore

A male mountain gorilla is called a silverback.

Where Do They Live?

Mountain gorillas live in four national parks in Central Africa in the countries of the Democratic Republic of Congo (DRC), Rwanda and Uganda.

Key

Oceans and Seas

Land

Mountain Gorilla Habitats

AFRICA

Indian Ocean

Atlantic Ocean

Why Are They in Danger?

The biggest threat to mountain gorillas is habitat destruction. War and **conflict** in the DRC and Rwanda has led to illegal deforestation, poaching and construction of buildings and houses. This has caused habitat loss and, as a result, a huge decrease in mountain gorilla numbers.

MORE THAN 100,000 PEOPLE LIVE IN THE AREAS WHERE MOUNTAIN GORILLAS ARE FOUND. THESE HUMAN POPULATIONS THREATEN THE NATURAL HABITATS OF GORILLAS.

HOW ARE THEY BEING PROTECTED?

War and conflict have made conservation very difficult. But, despite this, the population of mountain gorillas has increased from 620 in 1989 to around 880 today. In 1991, the International Gorilla Conservation Programme (IGCP) was created in order to protect the habitats that mountain gorillas depend on for their survival. The IGCP have worked with governments to support **reforestation** projects and increase the number of anti-poaching patrols.

Park rangers patrolling inside Virunga National Park, DRC

THE POPULATIONS OF MOUNTAIN GORILLAS THAT LIVE IN THE VIRUNGA AND VOLCANOES NATIONAL PARKS HAVE GROWN BY 14% IN THE LAST 12 YEARS BECAUSE OF CONSERVATION EFFORTS.

ETHIOPIAN WOLF

FACTFILE

Number Living in the Wild: Less than 500

IUCN Status: Endangered

Scientific Name: *Canis simensis*

Weight: Up to 20 kg

Size: Up to 62 cm tall

Life Span: Up to 10 years

Habitat: Mountainous and rocky habitats at high altitudes of 3,000 m and above

Diet: Carnivore

Ethiopian Wolf

Where Do They Live?

Ethiopian wolves only live in seven areas of the **highlands** of Ethiopia, in East Africa.

Key

Oceans and Seas
Land
Ethiopian Wolf Habitats

Indian Ocean

AFRICA

Ethiopia

Atlantic Ocean

WHY ARE THEY IN DANGER?

One of the main reasons the Ethiopian wolf is endangered is habitat loss caused by **agriculture** and the need to clear land for **livestock**. This has meant that the Ethiopian wolf has had to move to higher habitats, which have much harsher weather and less food. Another serious threat to the population are diseases passed on from dogs, such as rabies, which can easily kill entire Ethiopian wolf populations.

The Bale Mountains National Park, Ethiopia, where over half of the population of Ethiopian wolves live.

How Are They Being Protected?

The Ethiopian Wolf Conservation Programme (EWCP) was created in 1995 to help protect Ethiopian wolves. To do this, they employed people from local communities as 'Wolf Ambassadors'. The EWCP has also funded the **vaccinations** of domestic dogs to stop the spread of rabies to Ethiopian wolves. The government has also legally protected 87% of the Ethiopian wolf's habitats.

An Ethiopian wolf in the Bale Mountains National Park, Ethiopia

BLACK RHINOCEROS

FACTFILE

Number Living in the Wild: 5,000–5,500

IUCN Status: Critically Endangered

Scientific Name: *Diceros bicornis*

Weight: 900–1,400 kg

Size: Approximately 1.6 m tall

Life Span: 35 to 40 years

Habitat: Grassland, savannah, woodland and wetland

Diet: Herbivore

Black Rhinoceros

Where Do They Live?

Black rhinoceroses live in southern and eastern Africa, in the countries of South Africa, Zimbabwe, Kenya, Tanzania and Namibia.

Key

Oceans and Seas

Land

Black Rhinoceros Habitats

AFRICA

Indian Ocean

Atlantic Ocean

AROUND 40% OF ALL BLACK RHINOCEROSES LIVE IN SOUTH AFRICA.

Why Are They in Danger?

Much like the African elephant, the black rhinoceros is critically endangered because it is often killed by poachers for its horns. Black rhinos grow two horns which, like elephant tusks, are also extremely valuable. Rhino horns are often used in traditional Chinese medicine or as a **symbol** of wealth and success.

While poachers remain the biggest threat to the black rhino, habitat loss caused by the rising human population has also caused their numbers to decrease.

HOW ARE THEY BEING PROTECTED?

To prevent the killing of black rhinos for their valuable horns, many countries have cut the horns off some of their rhino population to stop poachers from killing them. However, this is expensive, takes a long time and poachers will still often kill dehorned rhinos for the tiny pieces of horn that are left. Also, laws to protect the black rhino and their habitats have become much stricter. Conservation efforts have caused the rhino's population to increase from around 2,400 to 5,000 in the last 20 years.

A De-Horned Black Rhino

EVEN THOUGH THE BLACK RHINO POPULATION IS SHOWING SIGNS OF RECOVERING, THEIR NUMBERS HAVE STILL DECREASED BY 97.6% OVERALL IN THE LAST 50 YEARS.

19

AFRICAN LION

FACTFILE

Number Living in the Wild: Less than 30,000

IUCN Status: Vulnerable

Scientific Name: *Panthera leo*

Weight: 150–230 kg

Size: Approximately 1.2 m tall

Life Span: 10 to 14 years

Habitat: Grassland, savannah and open woodland

Diet: Carnivore

Male African Lion

Where Do They Live?

African lions live in Angola, Botswana, Mozambique, Tanzania, the Central African Republic, South Sudan and other parts of **sub-Saharan** Africa.

Key

- Oceans and Seas
- Land
- African Lion Habitats

AFRICA

Indian Ocean

Atlantic Ocean

WHY ARE THEY IN DANGER?

Lion families, called prides, need large areas of land in order to find enough **prey**. The more the human population grows, the less space lions have and the more that lions and humans come into contact and conflict with one another. For example, lions may kill and eat farmers' animals because it is an easily caught meal and, in turn, a farmer may **retaliate** and kill the lion to protect the animals on their farm. Conflicts like these are the biggest cause of lion deaths in Africa.

In south-eastern Tanzania over 400 people were killed by lions from 1997 to 2007.

How Are They Being Protected?

Wildlife organisations are working with local communities to educate people about how important lions are to the environment and to the local **economy** because of **wildlife tourism**. As well as taking important steps to protect the lions, protection has been provided to the villages too, to keep both the people and the animals safer.

THE POPULATION OF AFRICAN LIONS HAS DECREASED BY AROUND 42% BETWEEN 1996 AND 2017.

AFRICAN PENGUIN

FACTFILE

Number Living in the Wild: Around 50,000

IUCN Status: Endangered

Scientific Name: *Spheniscus demersus*

Weight: Up to 3.6 kg

Size: Around 60–70 cm tall

Life Span: Between 10–27 years

Habitat: Marine habitats on the coastline and islands of south-west Africa

Diet: Carnivore

THE AFRICAN PENGUIN IS ALSO KNOWN AS THE JACKASS PENGUIN.

Where Do They Live?

African penguins live in large groups called colonies, which are found in 28 locations on the coast and islands off southern Africa.

AFRICA

Indian Ocean

Atlantic Ocean

Key

- Oceans and Seas
- Land
- African Penguin Habitats

Why Are They in Danger?

The population of African penguins is declining very rapidly because of food shortages caused by fishing. Two of the African penguin's main sources of food (anchovies and sardines) are caught by humans using a modern method called purse-seining. This allows fishing boats to catch huge numbers of fish at one time. The method has been so successful that some African penguins have **starved**.

An example of a fishing boat using the purse-seine method of catching fish.

POLLUTION CAUSED BY TWO SERIOUS OIL SPILLS IN 1994 AND 2000 ARE ESTIMATED TO HAVE KILLED 30,000 AFRICAN PENGUINS.

HOW ARE THEY BEING PROTECTED?

The African penguin population is decreasing so fast that immediate conservation measures have been put in place. Many areas the African penguins call home are now protected under law. For example; Nambia protects almost 10,000 square km of ocean in southern Nambia. South Africa has also put in place 20 km 'no take' zones. No take zones are protected marine areas where fishing is not allowed. The survival rate of the African penguin has increased in these areas.

CONSERVATION EFFORTS IN AFRICA

Many steps have already been taken to protect wildlife and conserve habitats throughout Africa, but much more can still be done to save endangered animals from extinction.

Laws and Governments

Much progress has been made to protect African wildlife and habitats by creating legally protected spaces such as national parks or nature reserves. For example, 30% of Zambia's land is protected from humans living or building on it and it has 20 national parks that are legally protected. However, there are over 54 countries in Africa and they all have their own different laws and governments so it can take a long time for change to happen.

Governments have also worked to make punishments for breaking laws much stricter. For example, the Kenyan government has created harsher sentences for poachers. Previously, those caught killing animals illegally in Kenya could be fined up to 700 pounds. Now they can be fined up to 170,000 pounds and put in prison for life! Government organisations are also providing funds for law **enforcement**. This includes providing more park rangers and giving them better training to help to keep wildlife safer.

DESPITE RECENT EFFORTS TO CONSERVE THE HABITATS OF THE AFRICAN ELEPHANT, AROUND 70% OF THEM ARE NOT PROTECTED BY LAW.

COMMUNITIES

Speaking to communities directly about how to help to conserve the wildlife within an area is extremely important. For example, an organisation called the Lion Guardians has helped protect Africa's lions by speaking to the Maasai people. Traditionally, young male members of the Maasai people have killed lions as a sign of bravery. The organisation has given jobs to these members as 'lion guardians'. The 'lion guardians' are paid to protect the lions. They do this by resolving conflicts between wildlife and humans, checking on the lion population and helping their own communities live peacefully alongside them.

Members of the Maasai Community

Wildlife tourists like these ones are here to help to protect wildlife and conserve habitats.

Education

Education is one of the most important tools we have to help endangered animals. Teaching people about wildlife and the important part it plays can often be enough to change people's attitudes. For example, many wildlife organisations, charities and governments are investing in projects to make wildlife tourism a source of income for local communities. Many will no longer be able to continue their farming practices, which damage the land that needs to be protected. Projects like these protect people as they provide a regular source of income and protect wildlife and habitats too.

HOW CAN I MAKE A DIFFERENCE?

1 CAMPAIGN WITH AN ORGANISATION

Wildlife organisations such as WWF and Greenpeace have helped to save many endangered species, and even convince countries to change their laws through campaigning.

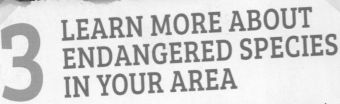

2 DONATE TO A CHARITY YOU BELIEVE IN

You can usually donate as little or as much as you want. Most charities show you how your donations are helping to make a difference.

3 LEARN MORE ABOUT ENDANGERED SPECIES IN YOUR AREA

One of the most important ways to protect endangered species is by understanding the threats that they face. Visit a local wildlife refuge, national park or reserve, or join a local wildlife organisation.

4 ADOPT AN ANIMAL

Your donation will normally go to feeding and looking after the animal that you have adopted. You'll usually get an adoption certificate and regular updates on how your animal is doing.

5 HELP TO RAISE AWARENESS BY TALKING TO OTHERS

It is important that we all talk about issues that may threaten wildlife throughout the world. By talking about these issues, it can help to make people aware of how they may be affecting wildlife and tell them how they can help.

6 VOLUNTEER AT A LOCAL WILDLIFE CHARITY OR SHELTER

It is not only endangered animals who need our help; we should help to take care of all the animals in the world.

FIND OUT MORE

To find out more about endangered species in Africa and what you can do to get involved with conservation efforts, visit:

African Conservation Foundation (ACF)
www.africanconservation.org

African Wildlife Foundation (AWF)
www.awf.org

Convention on International Trade in Endangered Species (CITES)
www.cites.org

International Union for Conservation of Nature (IUCN)
www.iucnredlist.org

World Wide Fund for Nature (WWF)
www.worldwildlife.org

To discover more about other endangered animals around the world, take a look at more books in this series:

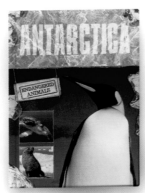

Antarctica, Endangered Animals
Grace Jones (BookLife, 2018)

Asia, Endangered Animals
Grace Jones (BookLife, 2018)

Australia, Endangered Animals
Grace Jones (BookLife, 2018)

Europe, Endangered Animals
Grace Jones (BookLife, 2018)

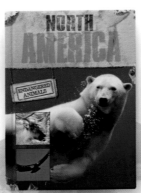

North America, Endangered Animals
Grace Jones (BookLife, 2018)

South America, Endangered Animals
Grace Jones (BookLife, 2018)

QUICK QUIZ

1. HOW MANY MOUNTAIN GORILLAS ARE LIVING IN THE WILD?

2. WHAT IS THE SCIENTIFIC NAME OF THE BLACK RHINOCEROS?

3. WHAT NAME IS THE AFRICAN PENGUIN ALSO KNOWN BY?

4. WHAT SORT OF HABITAT DOES THE ETHIOPIAN WOLF LIVE IN?

5. HOW MUCH DO ADULT AFRICAN ELEPHANTS WEIGH?

6. WHAT IS THE IUCN CONSERVATION STATUS OF THE MOUNTAIN GORILLA?

For answers see the bottom of page 32.

GLOSSARY

adapted	changed over time to suit different conditions
agriculture	the practise of farming
altitudes	heights above sea level
captivity	animals that are cared for by humans and not living in the wild
carnivore	animals that eat other animals rather than plants
conflict	active disagreement
conservation	the practice of protecting or conserving a species and its habitats
deforestation	the action of cutting down trees on large areas of land
domestic	relating to a particular country, not international
economy	the way trade and money is controlled and used by a country or region
enforcement	making something happen using rules and laws
environment	the natural world
governments	groups of people with the authority to run countries and decide their laws
habitats	the natural environments in which animals or plants live
herbivore	an animal that only eats plants
highlands	an area of high or mountainous land

illegally	in a way forbidden by law
livestock	animals that are kept for farming purposes
marine	relating to the sea
meteorite	a piece of rock that successfully enters a planet's atmosphere without being destroyed
natural resources	useful materials that are created by nature
organisation	an organised group of people who work together for a shared purpose
poaching	the act of the illegal capturing or killing of wild animals
population	the number of people living in a place
prey	animals that are hunted by other animals for food
reforestation	the action of replanting an area with trees
retaliate	react to someone or something because they have done something to you
savannah	a flat area of land covered with grass and with few trees
settlements	places people live permanently, like villages or towns
species	a group of very similar animals or plants that are capable of producing young together
starved	to have died or suffered from hunger
sub-Saharan	the geographical area that is below the Sahara desert in Africa
symbol	to stand for or represent someone or something
vaccinations	treatments to stop certain diseases affecting people
wildlife tourism	the actions and industry behind attracting people to visit new places to see wildlife

1. Around 880 **2.** Diceros bicornis **3.** Jackass penguin
4. Mountainous and rocky habitats **5.** Between 3.5 to 6.5 tonnes **6.** Critically endangered